Basic Fish Cooking Methods

A No Frills Guide for
Preparing Fresh Fish

Renee Shelton

i

ISBN: 1456492993
ISBN-13: 978-1456492991

DEDICATION

To my husband who is my best fishing buddy
To my children who make all my days a joy.
Thanks.

CONTENTS

ACKNOWLEDGMENTS

Thanks to everyone who helped put this book together.
Your support and encouragement have been invaluable.

1
INTRODUCTION

Basic Fish Cooking Methods: A No Frills Guide to Preparing Fresh Fish and Seafood

We like to fish. When fishing, we primarily catch-and-release, but keep some fish that we know we'll consume. Our family also lives close to several fresh fish markets that provide our region with excellent fresh fish and seafood. Living in Southern California gives our family the opportunity to scout out great fish markets locally for fresh fish, and fish for local freshwater and saltwater species.

Since I do cook a lot of fish for my family to eat, I am asked frequently what are the best methods to cook certain fish, how to do a technique found in a book. I wanted to provide a cookbook with basic methods of fish cooking, rather than simply a bunch of fancy recipes. This book is a no frills guide for purchasing and preparing fish using basic cooking methods.

What will you find in this book? In this book, you'll find basic guidelines for purchasing fresh fish or seafood including what to look for, like the odor and texture of the fish or the color of the gills. I also listed basic procedures for cooking fish and seafood. They are essentially recipes with no ingredients.

Create your own recipes with these procedures and the fish you have. And if you are looking for some different recipes to add to your own collection, I've provided family favorites that I cook at home. All the recipes have been formulated to create four to six servings, and can be adjusted up or down easily. I thank my family for being the ultimate taste testers for all the recipes.

There are many varieties of fish out there to choose from, whether you catch your own fish for dinner or purchase it from your favorite fishmonger or supermarket. And no matter where the fish came from, it is all cooked with the same methods and techniques.

Everyone knows incorporating fish into the diet is good for health reasons, but using the proper cooking methods and techniques for preparing your favorite varieties will make it easier to eat fish on a regular basis. Why? Fish and seafood taste better when they are prepared properly.

You don't need fancy ingredients or equipment to pan fry a fillet, or oven broil a steak. You just need instructions on the proper way to carry out the tasks.

Enjoy!

Renee Shelton

PART ONE:

BASIC TERMS FOR PURCHASING
AND PREPARING FISH AND SEAFOOD

2
BASIC FISH ANATOMY

It is important to know the different parts to a fish for cutting your own fillets and steaks.

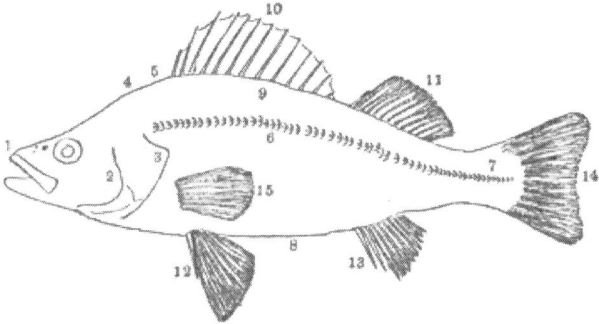

Using the guide above, here are the basic parts to a fish:
1. The Snout.
2. Preopercle, sometimes referred to as POP, which are the bones on either side of the head.
3. Opercle, or the gill coverings.
4. The Nape of the fish, at the 'neck'.
5. The Shoulder of the fish.
6. This long line running the length of the fish on the sides is the Lateral Line, and can be curved or straight or entirely gone, depending on the variety of fish.
7. This is the Base of the Caudal Fin.
8. The Ventral area is the actual abdomen or belly part (or lower half) of the fish.
9. The Dorsal area is the actual back area (or top part) of the fish.

10. In the case of fish having more than one fin, the first fin would be The First Dorsal Fin; otherwise the top fin would be the Dorsal Fin.
11. The fin behind the first dorsal fin would be The Second Dorsal Fin.
12. The Ventral Fin is the bottom fin.
13. The Anal Fin is the bottom back fin.
14. The Caudal Fin is the tail fin of the fish.
15. The Pectoral Fins are the fins on either side of the fish's body.

3
MARKET FORMS OF FISH: TERMINOLOGY

There are several market forms of fish that are available to the consumer. When you see fish laid out on ice at the supermarket or at the local fishmonger, it will either be whole or already cut up and ready for cooking.

Some recipes will call for a certain cut of fish (think steak or pan dressed). If you don't see it laid out for you, ask for it. If you caught the fish yourself, you'll have to do the work but you'll also get to keep the scraps of bone and other parts that can be used for fish stock.

The market forms will sometimes vary from region to region, or from market to market. Some terms may be familiar and some will be new. Some forms will only be found in wholesale markets since the cuts are so large.

All the terms are commonly known among most professional chefs and some of them may not apply to the retail market, but now you'll have knowledge of each.

Listed by order of processing or size.

- *Round*: Whole fish, unprocessed
- *Headed*: Whole fish with head removed
- *Drawn*: Whole fish with entrails/viscera removed
- *Split*: Entrails/gills/roe removed, cut from the throat to the tail or vent
- *Dressed*: Entrails removed, scaled—head and tail may or may not be removed

- *Pan Dressed*: Entrails removed, scaled, head/fins/tail removed
- *Roast*: Whole cuts of large fish, generally the back end part
- *Block*: Large dress fish section—crosswise cut
- *Chunk*: Smaller dress fish section—crosswise cut
- *Loin*: Backbone portions, longitudinal cut of meat, size depends on fish, used with tuna
- *Steak*: Cross-sectional slices, straight cut of whole fish, generally thick
- *Fillet*: Cuts of sides of fish, may or may not have skin and bones attached
- *Butterflied Fillet*: Sides of fish joined at back/belly, backbone generally removed if attached at back
- *Fletches*: Half fillets of larger fish
- *Slices*: Sections of a large fillet
- *Scallops*: Thin sections/slices of a fillet
- *Sticks*: Cross section of a slice of fish

4
GUIDELINES FOR PURCHASING FRESH FISH

A couple of hallmarks of a whole, fresh fish are that it has a clean, ocean smell and that the flesh is firm. Bright eyes are another clue. But there are other things to look for when purchasing fresh fish, whether whole or in fillets, at both the fish market and the fish section at the local supermarket.

Don't take the seller's word that the fish is fresh. Carefully look over the fish or seafood yourself before purchasing to ensure it is fresh. If the fish is whole, look for obvious signs of age, such as dull, sunken eyes or a strong odor. Fish already cut into fillets or steaks will have a firm-feeling, brightly colored flesh.

It is important to purchase quality fish so that you are preparing food safe to prepare and safe for your family to eat.

Things to Look For When Purchasing Fresh Fish and Seafood

Odor/Smell
Always check the smell from fresh fish. The odor should be fresh smelling, without a strong 'fishy' odor. If it is a saltwater variety, the fish should smell of the ocean. Freshwater fish should also have a mild smell. Avoid those fish with a very strong odor as the flesh may have already started decomposing.

Firm Flesh, Stiff Fins, Tight Scales
The flesh should be firm and elastic, where it will spring back if touched with a finger or thumb. Avoid whole fish where the flesh leaves a visible 'dent' when you lightly press the flesh with your finger. If it is whole and the fins are present, check the fins which are an important clue. The fins should be firm and feel stiff.

Check the scales; they should be tightly clung to the skin. Avoid fish where the scales are clearly falling off and very loose. Filleted fish or fish steaks will be bright and moist. Avoid fish steaks and fish fillets that seem to be dried around the edges or where the flesh is discolored.

Eyes and Gills
The eyes of a whole fresh fish will be bright and firm, not sunken in and dried. The eyes will still be up with bright black pupils. Avoid those fish with sunken in and dull-colored eyes. The gills of the fish will also be bright, and the color red.

Check How the Fish Is Kept
Quality vendors will keep fish properly. Fresh, whole fish need to be on ice: on top of the ice, not sitting in melted ice water. Avoid those fish that are sitting inside what looks like a water bath. Fish need to be on top of ice in a self draining system to catch any melted runoff.

5
BASIC COOKING METHODS:
DRY HEAT AND MOIST HEAT

There are two basic methods of cooking: the dry heat method and the moist heat method. This applies to everything being cooked: meats, fish & seafood, and produce.

Within these two methods are many different techniques utilized to both cook the fish for optimal flavor and the best texture. Lean and fatty fish both have their favored techniques, and delicate and firm-fleshed fish will have theirs.

When choosing a technique for fish and seafood, think about the actual method with which it will be cooked. For fish, many different cooking techniques are used, but there are several that make up the majority of all recipes: pan frying, sautéing, poaching, simmering, deep frying, baking, and broiling.

What is the Dry Heat Cooking Method?
Dry heat cooking is basically cooking the fish or seafood by surrounding it by dry heat or fat, without moisture. This can be done on the stove top, in the oven, or on the barbeque.

Oven baking is a classic example of the dry heat cooking method using air in the oven. Deep fat frying is a classic example of the dry heat cooking method using fat on the stove top. The fish or seafood is cooked by the hot air or the hot fat that surrounds it.

What is the Moist Heat Cooking Method?
Moist heat cooking involves cooking the fish or seafood in a liquid such as a broth, seasoned water, or even its own juices. Poaching, steaming, and braising are all moist heat methods. The fish is cooked by the hot liquid that surrounds it, or the moisture it produces, like *fish en papillote*.

6
MENU DESCRIPTIONS
FOR POPULAR FISH RECIPES

A menu at a fish house or seafood restaurant, or any restaurant for that matter, will often have titles with no descriptions. Often, these are left out since the methods of preparation are universal to both the chef and the customer.

Here are descriptions of popular fish preparations on menus and in cookbooks.

- *Croquettes*: This is where fish is mixed with other ingredients and formed into small shapes and deep fried until golden. They are often rolled in an egg wash and crumb mixture to give a nice coating on the outside.
- *Deviled*: Mustard is generally used in the preparation and in the ingredient list, by way of dry mustard or prepared mustard.
- *En Papillote*: This dish has a serving size of fish topped with aromatic vegetables and spices or seasonings, and drizzled with a bit of white wine or other liquid (or no liquid at all)— all contained in a piece of parchment paper folded up to seal, and cooked in the oven without opening it until it is served. The baking will steam and cook the fish and vegetables in the oven. It is often opened tableside.
- *Fines Herbes*: The interpretation can be broad, but the fish is generally prepared or served with a variety of fresh herbs that are chopped or left whole for garnish.

- *Florentine*: Florentine is used with a wide variety of fish and seafood. While the chef's or cook's interpretation can vary widely, a dish with the word 'Florentine' in it generally contains spinach and a cheese or cream sauce.
- *Gratin*: This is another dish with a wide interpretation made by the cook or cookbook, but generally consists of a topping, such as bread crumbs, cooked on top to brown and give dimension to the dish.
- *Meuniere*: This dish consists of a floured and pan fried fish fillet that is served with a pan sauce made with browned butter and fresh parsley or other herbs. Often lemon is added for flavor.
- *Newburg*: This dish is prepared with cream, and served either over a pastry shell, toast points or pasta.
- *Mornay*: This is served with a Mornay sauce, which is a very creamy sauce made with different cheeses, such as Parmesan, Gruyere and Cheddar.
- *Thermidor*: This is a rich seafood dish prepared with cream, served in the shell (such as lobster meat placed back in its shell) or pastry shells and toast points. Thermidor is oftentimes finished with an alcohol such as brandy or thickened with egg yolks.
- *Vin Rouge*: This fish dish is served with a red wine sauce, or is poached in a red wine fumet

7
SPICE MIXTURES: FLAVORING FISH FOR ALL COOKING METHODS

Spice mixtures are used for both seafood and fish rubs, but also to flavor the sauces they are served with. They can be purchased in small containers, in bulk forms, or even be made at home.

Here are descriptions of popular spice blends used in the kitchen for fish and seafood recipes.

- *Garam Masala*—an exotic spice mixture containing such spices as cumin, nutmeg, cardamom, cinnamon, and black or white peppercorns. Garam masala can be very spicy or mild, just read the labels for the ingredient list before purchasing.
- *Curry Powder*—a popular blend of spices, generally containing coriander, ginger, fennel seed, turmeric, cumin, cinnamon, clove, mustard, nutmeg, and hot pepper for heat. The blend varies greatly from brand to brand, and can be very mild or intensely hot, especially if it is a homemade recipe.
- *Chili Powder*—a mixture of dried chilies and other dried spices, like cumin, garlic powder, ground oregano, paprika, turmeric, and sometimes cocoa powder.
- *Chinese Five Spice*—this has a slightly sweet, licorice flavored taste due to the fennel and aniseed inside it. It typically has a blend of five

different spices: aniseed, star anise, cloves, cinnamon, and fennel seeds. Other recipes will add different spices for different flavors, such as allspice or ginger, and may contain more than five spices.

- *Quatre-Epices (French Four Spice)*—from the French, this contains peppercorns, nutmeg, cloves and ginger. While many recipes contain only four basic spices, others will add cinnamon and/or allspice, or other spices for different flavors.

PART TWO:
BASIC DRY HEAT COOKING METHODS

What are the basic dry heat cooking methods used for fish cookery? This book will highlight and describe how to prepare fish and seafood by baking, oven broiling, pan frying, pan searing, sautéing, and deep frying. All cook fish and seafood without the introduction of liquid.

8
BAKING AND BROILING:
SIMILAR BY DIFFERENT COOKING METHODS

Baking and broiling are two ways to cook fish and seafood in the oven. The main difference between the two? One cooks food by hot air, and the other is a direct heating technique. Both methods are great, and both are healthy choices for cooking fish and seafood.

Baking is a technique that cooks food in the oven by surrounding the fish and seafood with hot air. The food is placed in the middle of the oven with the heating element on the bottom of the oven. The air in the oven space heats up and cooks the fish with the surrounding hot air.

This contrasts with the broiling technique, also an oven-based dry cooking method. Broiling is a technique that is actually similar to barbequing. The heat comes from one source (above the food) and the door is generally left open during cooking to keep the element on.

During baking, the heating element will turn on and off, keeping the air temperature at a constant and even one. With broiling it is important to keep the element on during the entire cooking time.

Some ovens will shut the heating element off after a certain temperature has been reached, which is why keeping the door open ajar slightly on some models ensures the top heating element stays on. Refer to your oven manual for details on oven broiling.

With broiling, the food is generally placed close to the heat source, and the food is cooked only on one side. Therefore, turning the fish or seafood over is necessary during oven broiling to brown all sides, if you want both sides to be browned.

During broiling, splattering may occur if the food is placed very close to the elements. Always watch the food carefully when oven broiling to prevent burning of the fish, or sparks from the element.

Ensure the pans used for both baking and broiling are oven-safe for the method being used. Some pans are oven-safe for baking, but will shatter or warp if placed close to the oven broiling heating element.

9
OVEN BAKING
COOKING PROCEDURE AND TIPS

Fish cooking tips: Oven baking basics

Oven baking is a classic way to cook fish. Here are some tips when oven baking.

- Use a rack for breaded fish fillets; it lifts them up off the baking dish to help ensure a crispy crust.
- When oven baking on a sheet pan, fish fillets may need to be turned over once during baking, to evenly brown both sides.
- Always preheat the oven before baking the fish.

Oven Baking Cooking Procedure

Basic Procedure for Oven Baking Fish

1. Preheat the oven to moderate heat. Temperatures between 350 degrees F and 375 degrees F are recommended for larger cuts of fish or whole fish to ensure even baking. Higher temperatures can be used for smaller or thinner cuts of fish without drying out the fish or toughening the texture.
2. Cut the fish as recommended in the recipe. Season the fish with salt and pepper, or with other herbs or spice mixtures.
3. Place the fish on a baking pan that has been lightly greased, and brush each fillet with a little melted butter or drizzle with oil, like an olive oil or a flavored or infused oil. Alternately, dip the

fish fillets or cut-up fish in a little melted butter and place on the baking sheet.

4. Bake in the oven, uncovered, until the fish flakes and tests done.
5. Serve.

10
OVEN BROILING
COOKING PROCEDURE AND TIPS

Fish cooking tips: Oven broiling basics

Oven broiling is a healthy way to cook fish fillets. The method consists of the heat coming from above rather than below. Here are some tips when oven broiling.

- Keep the door open ajar slightly. This will keep the heating element on, and help you to watch what is being broiled. Refer to your oven's operating manual for optimum broiler settings.
- Keep your foods at an even height. Foods very tall will brown much faster than those at a lower height.
- Lean fish will generally require a brush of melted butter or vegetable oil over the top.

Oven Broiling Cooking Procedure

Basic Procedure for Oven Broiling Fish

1. Preheat the broiler element in the oven (the top heating element). Don't use the salamander feature, if you have one installed in your oven. The salamander is simply used to brown an item prior to serving.
2. Cut the fish as recommended in the recipe, but generally thinner cuts are best used in the broiling technique. Thicker cuts should be butterflied or split open. A classic example is

lobster: splitting open a lobster prior to oven broiling.

3. Season the fish with salt and pepper, or other spice blends. Be careful what you sprinkle on top as it may burn under the hot element.

4. Place the fish in a broiler pan or a broiler-safe pan. Brush or drizzle each fillet with melted butter or a bit of oil. This is for flavor, but also keeps the fish from drying out under the element.

5. Make sure everything that will be broiled is the same height and in even sizes for even cooking. Taller items will brown quicker or may burn before the other pieces are cooked through. The same goes with smaller or thinner cuts.

6. Broil in the oven, uncovered, until the fish flakes and tests done. Thicker cuts of fish may require a flipping during broiling to finish cooking.

7. Serve.

11
STOVE TOP DRY HEAT COOKING:
PAN FRYING, PAN SEARING, AND SAUTÉING

All three of these cooking techniques are dry heat cooking methods which are done in a pan on the stovetop.

Pan frying

Pan frying is cooking fish or seafood over a moderate heat, with a moderate amount of fat. Different recipes will call for vegetable oils, butter, and even shortening as the fat. Items that are pan fried are often breaded, battered, or coated heavily with crumbs or flour to create a crispy outer crust.

Sautéing
Sautéing is cooking fish in a small amount of fat, using higher heat. The fish is usually only lightly dusted. The key to sautéing is preheating the pan prior to adding the fish, and making sure the pan is not overcrowded. Overcrowding leads the pan to lower its temperature, resulting in a less crisp or browned finished dish.

Pan searing
Pan searing is cooking the fish fillet over moderately high heat with no coating, such as flour, cornmeal or crumbs. Fish is cooked plain, until browned on both sides, and until the fish fillet or fish steak is cooked as desired. Firm fleshed fish varieties are best for pan searing. The use of non-stick pans during pan searing is helpful, as well.

Culinary Terms for Pan Frying, Sautéing, and Pan Searing Cooking Methods

These terms are used frequently in pan frying, sautéing, and pan searing. They refer to either the coating on the outside, or ways to finish the dish.

- *Dredging:* Sautéed items will often call for a dredging of flour before they are added to the pan. It is simply dusting the fillet on both sides lightly in flour.
- *Clarified Butter*: If butter is to be used instead of oil in the frying pan, use clarified butter. This is where all the water and milk solids have been removed from the butter, and helps prevent the butter from burning in the pan.
- *Deglaze*: Recipes will sometimes call for a liquid, such as a wine, broth or fruit juice like lemon juice, to be added to pan after cooking the fish to help remove any browned bits. This is called deglazing, and this is often used as a sauce that is served with the fish.

What is Escabeche?

Escabeche is a dish where fully cooked sautéed or pan seared fish is placed for a period of time in an acidic mixture, like a marinade using a vinegar or a white wine as the base of the sauce. The fish can be served as a first course, as an appetizer, or even over lettuce for a flavorful main dish salad. The fish is generally pan seared or sautéed until cooked through, as a coating on the outside is not necessary. The marinade is poured over the fish, and allowed to come to room temperature. It is then refrigerated overnight and served cold.

12
DEEP FAT FRYING BASICS: CREATING A CRISPY COATING WHEN DEEP FRYING

Deep fat frying is when the fish is breaded or battered, and submerged in hot fat to cook. When a fish is correctly deep fat fried, there will be a minimum of oil absorbed, the center will be moist, and the coating will be crisp with a golden brown color.

Egg Wash

This is a mixture of beaten eggs and milk or water, and is the middle part of a typical three-part breading station comprising of flour for dredging, egg wash for holding on the crumb coating, and the crumb coating which can anything from bread or cracker crumbs to crushed cornflakes, or cornmeal.

13
STANDARD BREADING METHOD: PROTECTING BOTH THE FISH AND THE FAT

All crisp breading in deep fat frying begin with a proper coating. A standard breading method when done correctly is mess-free, and will consist of three separate components. When the fish or seafood is placed inside a deep fryer, it should be breaded or coated in batter for these main reasons:

1. It gives a crispy coating on the outside, improving flavor and appearance, and keeps the center of the fillet or seafood moist.
2. It protects the fat from the liquids and seasoning on the fish, and will ensure a longer life of the fat.
3. It protects the fish from absorbing too much fat.

Basic Components and Method for Breading

There are three basic components of breading: flour, egg wash, and the breading itself.

The fish is placed in the flour and given a thin coat. This thin coat of flour helps the egg wash stick, which in turn helps the final breading stick to the fish. It is helpful to keep your hands separate so the job isn't so messy. In other words, keep your dry hand dry, and your wet hand wet.

For example, when the fish is moved from plate to flour, turn it over and place it in the egg wash with one hand. Using the other, turn over and lift up to drain any excess liquid with the other hand. When the fish is placed in the breading, use the 'dry' hand to toss the breading around it, then flip it over to coat the other side. Place the breaded fish on a separate clean plate, and repeat with the rest of the fish.

14
DEEP FAT FRYING COOKING PROCEDURE AND TIPS

Tips for Deep Fat Frying:

Select an oil that is best for deep frying. Serve the fish immediately after frying for best result, and to keep the breading crisp. Here are two basic tips for deep fat frying.

1. The oil should be neutral flavored, and of good quality. A strongly flavored oil will end up passing its flavor onto the fish being fried. Some oils also perform better at higher temperatures than others, so always know the smoking point of the oil you are frying with.
2. Fry at the proper temperatures—350 degrees F to 375 degrees F is a good range. If it is too low, the fish will soak up the oil, and if it is too hot, the fish will burn on the outside before ever really cooking the center.

Deep Frying Cooking Procedure

Basic Procedure for Deep Frying Fish

1. Preheat the fryer with oil. Use the temperature setting recommended for the recipe, but most will have a temperature range that is between 350 degrees F and 375 degrees F.
2. Use a neutral flavored oil, and one suitable for deep fat frying. If a fryer will not be used, fill a saucepan or pot with the oil, but no more than

halfway full for safety reasons. You'll need just enough to cover the fish completely.

3. Prepare the breading ingredients, or make a batter for deep fat frying.
4. Coat the fish with the breading using the standard breading method, or dip in a batter. The fish may be seasoned before breading or dipping into the batter, or the flour that is used for dredging may be seasoned.
5. Place the fish in the hot fat, and fry until golden, and the fish tests done.
6. Drain, and then serve immediately.

15
PAN FRYING COOKING PROCEDURE

Pan Frying Cooking Procedure

Basic Procedure for Pan Frying Fish

1. Assemble the breading ingredients. If using the three step breading procedure, have a dish with flour, another dish with egg wash, and a third dish with your desired coating for the outside of the fish.
2. Preheat the pan over moderate heat with about 1/8 inch of vegetable oil. Use a pan large enough to allow easy turning of the fillets.
3. Bread the fish by dredging in flour first with one hand, and placing it in the egg wash. With the other hand turn the fillets over to coat both sides with the egg wash, and place it in the crumb coating. Using the flour dredging hand, turn the fillets over to coat both sides and place it in the hot pan. Using different hands for the dry coating and wet coating will make clean up easy.
4. Cook the fillets until they are browned on one side, then turn over and brown the other side. Continue to cook until the fish tests done in the center.
5. Remove and serve.

16
SAUTEING COOKING PROCEDURE

Sautéing Cooking Procedure

Basic Procedure for Sautéing Fish

1. Preheat the pan. Use a pan large enough to hold the fish or seafood in an even layer. The key to sautéing is to avoid overcrowding the pan, which will lead to a reduction in temperature in the pan when cooking.
2. Add in a small amount of oil, and swirl to cover the bottom.
3. Season the fish, then dredge lightly in flour, if using, for an even coat. Shake off any excess flour. You don't want a thick coat, just a nice even coating to help prevent sticking and finish the dish.
4. Place the fish in the pan and cook until browned on one side, then turn over and cook the other side. Sautéing generally involves quick cooking over a moderately high heat, so seafood, such as shrimp, makes a better choice for sautéing than larger fillets. Keep the pan at an even temperature for best results.
5. Remove the fish or seafood from the pan after the fish tests done, and serve.

17
PAN SEARING COOKING PROCEDURE

Pan Searing Cooking Procedure

Basic Procedure for Pan Searing Fish

1. Preheat pan over moderately high heat with a small amount of oil.
2. Season the fish and place it in the hot pan. Brown on the first side, then turn over and brown on the second side. Make sure the fillet is cooked before serving, and if not, place in a preheated oven to finish cooking. You want a pan seared fillet to be browned, but all the way cooked through as well. Some recipes, such as tuna loins, may call for the fish to be served raw in the center after searing. Pan searing larger loins will often call for the fish to be rolled in some kind of spice before cooking for flavor and texture.
3. This method is best for firm-fleshed fish. Very delicate fish may break up during pan searing.

PART THREE:
BASIC MOIST HEAT COOKING METHODS

What are the basic moist heat cooking methods used for fish cookery? This book will highlight and describe how to prepare fish and seafood by poaching or simmering. Both cook fish and seafood with the introduction of a liquid.

18
THE KEY DIFFERENCES
BETWEEN POACHING AND BOILING FISH

Poaching is a classical way to cook the fish in a hot liquid that is generally well-flavored. Poaching is a gentle form of cooking, which is perfect for the delicate nature of fish and seafood. Sometimes, boiling fish is used. This method is not often used, since it breaks up the meat and toughens most seafood.

The main difference between boiling and poaching is the temperature of the cooking liquid. Boiling will have rolling bubbles breaking the surface. Poaching is cooking the fish at lower temperatures.

19
THE KEY DIFFERENCES
SIMMERING AND BRAISING FISH

Simmering is a cooking method great for most fish or seafood. The seafood or fish fillets are allowed to cook in their own juices, or with a flavorful liquid that is introduced to the pan.

Very little liquid is used when simmering. Use the liquid from the cooking vegetables or ingredients in the pan, or simply from the seafood itself. A little wine, stock, or even lemon or lime juice is often added for flavor.

Simmering is generally a quick cooking method. It differs from braising in that the cuts of seafood are not browned before cooking. Braising is done both on the stove top and in the oven, is considered to be a moist version of baking, where the fish is cooked with a small amount of liquid.

20
THE KEY DIFFERENCES
POACHING AND SIMMERING FISH

Poaching and simmering are both moist heat cooking methods. The difference between the two? One is cooking a piece of fish at a very low temperature, usually between 160 degrees F and 185 degrees F, and the other is cooking the fish in its own juices or simmering in a small amount of liquid.

For poaching, the liquid should be flavorful and hot, but bubbles should not break the surface. Popular liquid choices for poaching fish are a fish stock, fumet, wine, light chicken or vegetable broth, or court bouillon. Special fish poachers are oftentimes used since they contain a rack for the fish to lie upon, and have handles to easily lift it from the liquid when it is done. Poaching is an excellent way to cook delicate fish.

The simmering cooking method is where the fish or seafood is cooked with vegetables or other ingredients, then the pan is covered and the fish is allowed to finish cooking. Sautéing the vegetables first before adding the fish to the pan is an easy way to introduce flavor to the fish fillets. Sometimes, other liquid is added to the pan or poured over the fish before it is covered.

21
WHAT IS A COURT BOUILLON?

A court bouillon is a flavorful liquid used to boil or poach fish. It can be made from many different ingredients, each to impart a different flavor, or made especially for different fish. It can be as simple as water with a bit of seasonings to flavor it, to a rich fish stock with white wine.

Here is a run down on the typical ingredients in a court bouillon, how a fish poacher pan is used, and a basic recipe for a court bouillon.

Ingredients in a Court Bouillon

The ingredients in any court bouillon will depend on the finished flavors of the dish. A basic court bouillon will contain a liquid, such as water or a very light vegetable stock, an acid, such as wine, lemon juice or a vinegar, and a flavoring such as herbs, spices, or chopped vegetables like celery or onions.

Using Fish Poacher Pans

Fish poachers come in different sizes and shapes. The most popular shaped fish poacher pan has a long and narrow rectangular shape, and fits a typical whole round fish, such as a trout. A diamond shape fish poacher has a kite shape to it, making it great for flat fishes such as a turbot or halibut.

Fish poachers have a removable rack that is placed on the bottom making it easy to set the fish inside the court bouillon, and then taking it out when it is finished. Removing the fish in this fashion prevents it from being broken up, and is great for platter presentation if the whole fish will be presented for dinner or a buffet table.

22
BASIC COURT BOUILLON RECIPE

Add in any flavoring to taste that you want for your fish, such as different herbs, vegetables like mushroom or onion trimmings, shallots, garlic, spices like star anise, fennel seed, or even caraway or cumin seeds. Substitute the vinegar for cider vinegar, lemon or lime juice or a dry white wine for the liquid.

Basic Court Bouillon Recipe

- 2 quarts water
- 1/2 cup white wine vinegar
- 1 onion, cut into 8 pieces
- 2 carrots, sliced into thick rounds
- 2 stalks celery, cut into pieces, including the leafy tops
- 1/2 cup roughly snipped fresh parsley
- 2 whole bay leaves
- 1 large sprig of fresh dill
- 1 small sprig of fresh thyme
- 6 to 8 whole black peppercorns
- 1 teaspoon to 1 tablespoon of salt, as desired, to taste

1. Bring the ingredients to a boil. Lower heat, and simmer for about 20 to 30 minutes.
2. Strain all the ingredients out of the liquid. The court bouillon can be used immediately, or cooled properly and used later in recipes.

23
POACHING COOKING PROCEDURE

Here are some tips when poaching:

- Make sure the liquid is well-flavored, and of good quality.
- The liquid should be hot, but bubbles shouldn't break the surface. The actual cooking temperature of the hot liquid should be between 160 degrees F and 180 degrees F. Water boils at 212 degrees F (at sea level). Higher temperatures will actual boil the fish, and may end up breaking up the delicate meat of the fish.
- Use a fish poacher if you have one available. Fish poachers are special pans that are large enough to hold large fillets or whole fish. They have a removable rack at the bottom that will easily lift the fish from the pot after the fish is cooked.

Poaching Cooking Procedure

Basic Procedure for Poaching Fish

1. Prepare the court bouillon, or gather the ingredients that will be used to poach the fish in, such as white wine, lemon juice, aromatic vegetables, and water.
2. Place the fish in the pan, and add the poaching liquid.
3. Set the poaching pan over low heat, and very slowly bring it up to a simmer. A thermometer will help in achieving the

correct temperature, and in keeping it there.

4. Cook the fish at the correct poaching temperature of a minimum of 160 degrees F and no greater than 180 degrees F.

5. Remove the fish from the poaching liquid when it tests done.

6. Fish can be served hot, or properly cooled down and served chilled.

24
SIMMERING COOKING PROCEDURE

Simmering Cooking Procedure

Basic Procedure for Simmering Fish

1. Heat a pan, and add in oil or butter as indicated by the recipe.
2. Sauté the vegetables or sauce ingredients over medium to medium high heat.
3. Add the fish, presentation side down, and add any flavoring liquid, such as a splash of wine or fish stock. Lower the heat.
4. Cover the pan, and simmer over low heat until the fish tests done. About halfway through cooking, turn the fish over, and check the cooking to ensure the heat isn't too high, and that the fish will not be overcooked.
5. Serve the fish with the simmered sauce.

PART FOUR:
RECIPES

RECIPES TO TRY

Here are several recipes to try that use the cooking methods above, or to be served with fish.

Oven Broiled Vermilion Rockfish with Kalamata Black Olives & Tomatoes

This recipe isn't limited to rockfish: use your favorite fish fillet for this recipe instead. I put everything into the same pan for an easy to prepare meal using the oven broiling cooking method.

Makes 4 servings.

- 4 vermilion rockfish fillets, about 4 to 5 ounces each (or use a whole fish, boned and scaled)
- 1 medium onion, chopped
- 2 medium tomatoes, chopped
- 8 to 10 whole pitted Kalamata olives
- 2 cloves garlic, crushed
- 1/4 cup dry white wine
- Olive oil
- 2 sprigs of fresh oregano or basil
- Salt and black pepper, to taste
- Chopped fresh parsley

1. Preheat the oven broiler setting to 425 degrees F.
2. Rub a little olive oil on the bottom of an oven-proof baking pan (image above uses a broiler-safe paella pan). Arrange the onions, tomatoes, olives and garlic on the bottom. Add the white wine over the top. Remove the oregano leaves from the sprigs and sprinkle over the vegetables.
3. Sprinkle a little salt and pepper over the fish fillets. Lay over the vegetables. Drizzle with a little bit of olive oil.

4. Place in the oven, about 4 inches from the broiler element. Broil until the fish tests done (flesh is opaque and flakes easily), about 10 to 15 minutes. Time will depend on the thickness of the fillet. Ensure all the fillets have finished cooking before serving.
5. Garnish with chopped fresh parsley.

Crispy Oven Baked Yellowtail with Garam Masala & Curry Spice

Coating fish in crushed cornflakes is a healthy way to serve baked fish with a crispy crust.

Makes 6 servings.

- 6 serving-sized fillets of yellowtail, bones removed
- 1 egg white
- 1 tablespoon water
- 1/2 teaspoon garam masala spice mixture
- 1/2 teaspoon curry powder
- 1 cup crushed corn flakes
- Olive oil

1. Preheat the oven to 400 degrees F.
2. Take the halibut fillets and pat them dry. Remove any bones if any are present.
3. In a shallow mixing bowl, beat the egg white and the water together. Add in the garam masala and curry spices, and blend well.
4. Place the crushed corn flakes in a separate shallow dish.
5. Take a yellowtail fillet and place it inside the egg white and spice mixture. Turn to coat both sides. Lift the fillet up to drain and allow any extra egg white mixture to drip back into the dish. Lay it in the crushed corn flakes, and turn to coat both sides.
6. Place the corn flake-crusted fillet on an oven baking rack. Repeat with the remaining fillets.
7. Drizzle each of the fillets with a little olive oil.

8. Bake in the oven until the crust is browned, and the fish flakes in the center, about 10 to 15 minutes depending on the thickness.
9. Remove and serve immediately.

Fresh Tuna Salad Nicoise

If fresh tuna isn't available, use canned solid albacore or solid light tuna, not the chunk versions.

Makes 4 servings.

- 12 ounces fresh poached tuna, flaked (see the following recipe)
- 12 ounces small red potatoes, steamed and cut in half
- 8 ounces fresh green beans, snapped, trimmed & steamed
- 4 small vine ripened tomatoes
- Hearts of Romaine, leaves washed, enough for 4 persons
- 4 hard boiled eggs, quartered
- 12 each whole pitted Kalamata olives
- Fresh tarragon leaves

Dressing:
- 1/3 cup olive oil
- 3 tablespoons red wine vinegar
- 1 garlic clove, pressed with a garlic press
- 1 teaspoon Dijon mustard

1. In four separate salad plates, arrange hearts of Romaine around plate.
2. For each plate: top with 3 ounces chilled poached tuna, 3 ounces red potatoes, 2 ounces green beans, 1 each tomato quartered, 1 each hard boiled egg, 3 Kalamata olives.
3. Whisk the olive oil, red wine vinegar, and pressed garlic together. Add in the Dijon mustard.

4. Drizzle a little bit of the dressing over each salad.
5. Top with tarragon leaves, and serve.

Court Bouillon Poached Tuna

Makes 4 servings.

- 12 ounces fresh tuna
- 1 celery stalk, chopped
- 1/2 small onion, chopped
- 1/2 lemon, for squeezing into the water
- Fresh ground black pepper

1. Use a fish poacher, or a pan large enough to allow the water to cover the top of the fish.
2. Add in about 1 quart of water, enough to just cover the fish, and add in the celery, onion, and lemon. Sprinkle in some freshly ground pepper.
3. Bring the temperature slowly up to poaching temperature, then poach the tuna until it tests done and flakes easy.
4. Remove the poached fish from the court bouillon and let it cool.
5. Flake gently and use for salads.

Halibut Veracruz with Lime, Tomatoes, and Chilies

This makes an easy and low-fat dinner menu item.

Makes 6 servings.

- 6 4-ounce pieces of halibut fillets
- 2 whole limes, halved
- 1 tablespoon canola oil
- 1 small onion, cut into slices
- 1 14-ounce can fire roasted diced tomatoes
- 1/2 cup sliced fresh red bell pepper
- 1/2 cup sliced fresh yellow bell pepper
- 1 tablespoon canned green chilies
- Salt and pepper to taste

1. Place the halibut fillets in a large dish. Remove any bones if present.
2. Squeeze two halves of limes over the fillets, turning each to coat with the lime juice. Set aside until later. Reserve the other two halves for later.
3. Heat the canola oil over medium heat in a large, shallow pan with a lid. Add in the onions and cook, stirring occasionally, for about 5 minutes until tender.
4. Add in the red and yellow sliced bell peppers, and cook for another 2 to 3 minutes, stirring often.
5. Pour in the canned tomatoes and green chilies. Take the halibut fillets, and place them presentation side down into the vegetables. Spoon some of the pepper and tomato mixture over the tops of the fillets.

6. Reduce heat to low, and cover.
7. Cook until the fish tests done and flakes easily, turning them over once during cooking.
8. Remove the halibut fillets from the pan, and place on a serving platter.
9. Squeeze the remaining lime juice into the tomato and pepper mixture, and season with salt and pepper.
10. Bring the mixture to a boil and reduce some of the liquid.
11. Serve the halibut and the Veracruz sauce together.

Swordfish Escabeche

Begin this recipe the day before you need it because it needs to sit in the refrigerator overnight to marinate.

Makes 4 servings.

- 1 pound swordfish, cut into 4 ounce pieces, see note below
- About 1/2 cup canola oil, divided
- 1 large onion, sliced
- 3 cloves garlic, chopped
- 1 cup white wine vinegar
- 1 teaspoon dried Mexican oregano
- 1/2 teaspoon dried basil leaves
- 1/2 teaspoon cracked black peppercorns
- 1/2 teaspoon salt
- 1/2 teaspoon dry mustard

1. Reserve 1/4 cup of the oil for the marinade, and set aside.
2. Prepare the swordfish. Swordfish steaks or fillets often come in large pieces. If the fishmonger gives a whole, 1 pound portion, cut in half crosswise, and then cut each in half lengthwise. This will make 4 thin fillets ready for pan searing. If the fish is already in long and thin fillets, just cut the pieces into smaller serving-sized portions.
3. Place a non-stick frying pan over moderately high heat. Add in about 1 to 3 tablespoons of oil to the pan, depending on the amount needed for the fish. Place prepared fish in the pan, and pan sear from 2 to 4 minutes, depending on the

thickness, and turn over to cook the other side. Cook until browned, and the fish flakes easily and tests done.

4. Transfer the seared swordfish into a glass dish that can be covered.

5. Wipe the frying pan, and add in the reserved 1/4 cup reserved oil. Add in the onions and cook over medium heat until softened, about 5 minutes.

6. Add in the garlic and stir for a minute until foamy, but do not let the garlic brown.

7. Add in the white wine vinegar and bring the mixture to a boil. Remove from heat and stir in the oregano, basil leaves, cracked peppercorns, salt, and mustard. Pour the mixture over the cooked swordfish, and stir around ensuring all the marinade has covered the fish.

8. Allow the fish to come to come to room temperature. Cover the dish, and then place in the refrigerator. Marinate overnight or at least 8 hours before serving.

9. Serve the fish at room temperature or chilled, as the main dish, an appetizer, or over greens as an entrée salad.

Oven Broiled Rosemary-Scented Salmon Steaks

This recipe uses a vinaigrette-style basting sauce for the salmon steaks as it broils.

Makes 6 servings.

- 6 serving-size salmon steaks
- Salt and back pepper
- 1 sprig fresh rosemary, the leaves stripped from the sprig
- 4 tablespoons white wine vinegar
- 6 tablespoons corn oil

1. Make a simple vinaigrette with the white wine vinegar, and stir in the rosemary leaves. Let stand at room temperature for at least an hour before using in the recipe.
2. Preheat the broiler oven setting to 425 degrees.
3. Strain the rosemary leaves from the vinegar and oil mixture, and reserve about 3 tablespoons for basting in a separate small bowl.
4. Season both sides of the salmon steaks with salt and pepper.
5. Dip the steaks into the rosemary-scented dressing, and place each on a broiler pan.
6. Broil for about 5 minutes, or until the salmon is slightly browned. Baste the steaks with some of the reserved dressing, turn each over, and continue broiling until the fish tests done, about 5 to 7 minutes.
7. Serve.

Sautéed Rockfish with Sweet Curry Mango & Coconut Sauce

Check the cans of coconut milk before using. You want coconut milk, not cream of coconut. A serving suggestion is to serve the fish with basmati rice and fresh watercress.

Makes 6 servings.

- 6 serving-sized portions of rockfish
- Oil, as needed for sautéing
- Salt and pepper for seasoning
- Sweet Curry Coconut Sauce (see the following recipe)

1. Preheat a sauté pan over medium-high heat, and drizzle a small amount of oil on the bottom. Swirl to coat the bottom.
2. Sprinkle each fillet with a little salt and pepper, and add in the fillets, presentation side down first.
3. Cook until light browned, about 5 minutes depending on the size of the fillets, then turn over. Continue cooking on the other side until browned, and the fish flakes easy and tests done.
4. Remove from the pan and transfer to a serving platter.
5. Serve the fish with some Sweet Curry Mango & Coconut Sauce.

Sweet Curry Mango & Coconut Sauce

This slightly sweet sauce is made from mango nectar and fresh ginger root. Yields about 1 1/2 cups of sauce.

- 1 cup mango nectar
- 1/2 cup plus 1/4 cup coconut milk (not cream of coconut)
- 1 small onion, chopped
- 1 heaping tablespoon of green curry paste
- 1 teaspoon chopped peeled ginger root
- 1 large garlic clove, cut in half

1. In a small saucepan, add in the mango nectar, 1/2 cup of coconut milk, chopped onion, curry paste, chopped fresh ginger root, and garlic clove.
2. Bring the mixture to a boil; then reduce to a simmer. Cook for about 20 minutes over a low simmer until the vegetables have softened and the liquid has been slightly reduced.
3. Place everything in a blender and carefully puree with the lid vented slightly until the mixture is smooth.
4. Wipe clean the same pan that was used to simmer the mixture. Set a fine mesh strainer over the saucepan, and pour the pureed sauce through the strainer, pressing down with a ladle or spatula until all the liquid has been extracted from the solids.
5. Add in the remaining 1/4 cup of coconut milk. Heat the mixture until hot, and serve.

Plain Beer Batter for Batter Fried Fish

*Use this for deep fried fish fillets or to batter-fry seafood.
This makes enough for a couple of pounds of fish.*

- 1 cup all purpose flour
- 2 large eggs
- Salt and pepper, as needed
- 2 12-ounce cans of beer

1. Whisk the flour to break up any lumps. Sprinkle in salt and pepper.
2. Beat the eggs together, and add them to the flour with the beer.
3. Stir until smooth.

ABOUT THE AUTHOR

Renee Shelton is a classically trained culinarian with a focus on baking, healthy cooking, and fish cookery. Her website FishingChef.com has basic methods for cooking fish and seafood, as well as recipes and rules for basic food safety when it comes to fish handling and seafood prep.

She is a pastry chef by trade, and is a small business owner. Her company specializes in pastry and culinary equipment, and she consults on a contract basis, worldwide. She is the creator of PastrySampler.com.

Renee frequently writes about food such as baking and cake decorating, fishing, and cooking with wholesome foods. Healthy cooking at home, she describes, is an effort to incorporate fresh, unprocessed ingredients into the family menus.

When she isn't testing recipes, writing about food, or reading business & trade journals, she can be found nurturing her family's many fruit trees and vegetables she grows at home, or finding all the hidden fishing spots in and around Southern California.

Her other books in print include:

12 Months of Mini Cakes: Fun Cakes for Kids to Create Throughout the Year With a Kid's Introduction to Sugar Craft
(Sand and Succotash Books, 2011, ISBN 9780984840120)

17311512R00039

Printed in Great Britain
by Amazon